SAY BYE-BYE TO YOUR DAY JOB IN 30 DAYS:

HOW I MAKE $5000 OR MORE PER MONTH IN PASSIVE INCOME WORKING FROM HOME

By

CRAIG LEBOWSKI

INTRODUCTION

I want to thank you and congratulate you for downloading this book.

Many people are completely unaware of what passive income is. Our society places such a large emphasis on active income that passive income is left in the trenches.

Passive income, otherwise known as residual income, is income that is received on a regular basis, with little or no effort needed to maintain it.

Can you imagine making money while you sleep (literally)?

If you answered yes to this question, then you are definitely reading the right book.

The truth of the matter is that a stream of passive income requires a lot of upfront work to create, but will generate income for days, months, and even years into the future.

Don't believe me?

I am still earning income from articles that I have published over 3 years ago! I wake up to earnings every single morning; those earnings come from revenue streams that I have set up in the past. I didn't lift a finger for 9 days when I was sick in bed...I still earned passive income, during this timeframe, from those revenue streams that I had set up years ago!

This is all possible, for you too, with the information that is found throughout this book.

Read the information, take action with regards to what you read, and reap the benefits of passive income for the rest of your life!

Thanks again for downloading this book, I hope you enjoy it!

TABLE OF CONTENTS

LEGAL NOTES

CHAPTER 1

AFFILIATE MARKETING

-WHAT IS AFFILIATE MARKETING?

Many people really do not have any idea what is affiliate marketing. Also known as Affiliate Site, this type of marketing would require the sellers to reward their affiliates every time they bring or refer a customer to buy their product. Usually, affiliates would give their visitors their own set of rewards in form of gift cards or cash. However, visitors must first complete an offer or refer other people to their site.

To make it simple, affiliate marketing is a partnership between one merchant and a couple of affiliates. This partnership is a win-win condition for both since they would get to share their revenues. The affiliate will get paid via commission basis. They would have to refer clicks and lead their visitor to the website of the merchant in case they want to buy the product offered by the latter.

To know more what is affiliate marketing or interested to be a part of an affiliate site, it is very important that you know the products that really interest you the most. Moreover, it is also vital that you know how to sell it the best way you can.

There were a lot of people who have tried to be an affiliate or a merchant. However, there are some who failed because they didn't have the qualities that a successful affiliate marketer should possess.

First of all, you have to be very patient. More often than not, they lose out and eventually become frustrated because of not enough patience. Before starting, you have to make sure that you have the desire to continue affiliate marketing.

You should also spend a lot of hard work as well. When you start affiliate marketing, you should put enough dedication, time, and of course, hard work. There would come a time that you even have to sacrifice your own sleep, change your working shift, and so many other things to give up just to continue on your websites. There's no such thing as easy cash especially if you are still beginning to take this venture.

Other than that, you also have to be creative at the same time. You should make a website that has a good content before you start putting the affiliate links at the content. If you have quality content, you can rest assure that more and more visitors will come back and read what's on your website.

-A Step By Step Guide on Becoming An Affiliate

When you first start out with the idea of making money on the internet, the better your skills are in a business sense the more likely you are to succeed. That is why you should be looking into getting some type of training or education on the business model you want to pursue; the only real business model worth pursuing online is affiliate marketing. Learning affiliate marketing skills with the wealthy affiliate university is the best cause of action anyone could take. Unfortunately most have their self-destruct button already set, and the countdown is in motion.

I'm not afraid to tell you that typing the keyword phrase (make money online) into a search engine is not going to help you one bit to learn how, but it is one way to empty your bank account in record time with the promise of earning wealth big time. Affiliate marketing is the only real way to earn a steady income online, learn affiliate marketing and you will be set for life, Let the wealthy affiliate university turn the tide of your demise and put you on the road to a professional career in affiliate marketing. Did you know that you can earn the bum marketing way without the need for websites or expensive web hosting?

Setting yourself up as an affiliate marketer is easy, there are thousands upon thousands of companies who are willing to share their profits with you, but without the affiliate training or education needed to be successful, getting one sale in this industry is most unlikely to happen.

In reality affiliate marketing is about pre-selling a product to a person who is in the market to buy that particular item. Doing a good job of this can pretty much guarantee you the sale and affiliate commission. Do it badly and the buyer will move on to someone else landing page. Bum marketing is a way to present products to buyers without the hassle of having to pay for web hosting and maintaining websites. There are things you need to learn before you can make it an effective way of earning a steady income online.

One of the Wealthy affiliate university subjects is teaching effective bum marketing, When done the right way bum marketing can be very profitable over time, with the added benefit of costing you nothing in advertising cost or web hosting fees, 100% profit the affiliate marketers dream come true. Learning how to market online for free is one of my favorite subjects, at the wealthy affiliate university.

Any sales that originate from your articles are 100% profit for you; this is how bum marketing works and is a favorite of 90% of professional affiliate marketers. Affiliate marketing works. It might seem too simple and basic to work, but it is a fact gaining a lot of ground and is increasing in popularity.

Like it or not there is no such thing as free education someone somewhere paid for yours in the past. And if you want to learn how to become a professional affiliate marketer you will have to learn how to get someone else to pay for your training and education again. Luckily for you, the wealthy affiliate university can teach you how to do that as well. By getting targeted people to the affiliate products sales page. Join now and start learning your way to a full-time professional affiliate marketing career.

-A Step By Step Guide on Setting Up An Affiliate Program

Affiliate marketing programs have become very popular today and there are many different types of programs out there, this gives you, the affiliate a great deal of choice in direction. Why are they now so popular? You will find that there are a number of explanations. The most probable reason, however, is possibly the fact that the benefits of affiliate marketing have become much clearer to many people who are looking at ways of earning money online.

In today's economy, both merchants and affiliates have found that affiliate marketing can be very beneficial for both of them. For the merchant, affiliate marketing offers them the chance to advertise their products at a much lower cost. On the other hand, for the affiliate, marketing the products of merchants has become an easy way of earning profits online by doing what they like most, and that is being creative while working from home.

Affiliate marketing has taken on a life of its own over the past few years of fame, and also, people's outlook about it has changed a great deal. Affiliate marketing is no longer considered as an alternative method for a merchant to advertise his or her products, or as a source of additional income for the affiliates. Merchants and affiliates alike now consider affiliate marketing as a main source of profit and revenue.

Affiliate marketing could be completely unknown to many people, but essentially, it's certainly not as very confusing as it looks or how individuals make it seem to be. So what is affiliate marketing? It's primarily promoting other people's goods for a commission; individuals give you cash for promoting their goods. There's no need to write a sales copy for the item, set up an internet purchasing site, or perhaps have a merchant account; all you have to do is to get that buyer to that product offer. Website marketing professional revealed an uncomplicated step-by-step guide to aid you clinch a win with this kind of online money making enterprise.

The initial thing to undertake is get a deal. You need to find an offer that is important, ethical, dependable, and that's likely to be exciting for your target audience. For the selection process, it's best to focus on the items which you have already bought and were actually happy with because you yourself understand that it's a profitable investment. When you have an industry similar to yourself, it's not going to be difficult pitching the item to them and they'll likely buy it too.

Second thing to do is to develop a bonus. It boosts your conversions and it makes your offer more attractive to customers. Additionally, everybody loves a bonus; individuals want added value for their income. With the bonus deals, your clients get something extra without having to pay extra and also this dynamic instantly becomes an advantage over your competitors. In case you have no idea how you can create a reward or where to get one, he shared exactly how he created Authority Leverage and modified it into an important product that his customers actually spend on.

Third step soon after developing a bonus would be to set up your offer to the open public. Come up with a short video that's detailed and that can stimulate the curiosity of the audience, then add a link underneath the video clip that will lead to a wider or full explanation of the "curiosity-trigger" of the video. The internet marketing and advertising specialist also emphasized the significance of a deadline for the product and the bonus that you might need to supply a link too. The due date, much like the "curiosity-trigger" raises conversions. At the bottom, present guidelines concerning the reward.

Fourth step is to create a brief message regarding the product - explain it and its particular rewards. Provide evidence of just how effective the item was for you and how it can be efficient for the visitors too. To wrap it up, send an obvious call to action having a time frame.

These are just the basic principles of how affiliate marketing programs can function for you. There are more methods to further maximize the profitability of such programs.

CHAPTER 2

KINDLE PUBLISHING

-PUBLISH YOUR CONTENT ON KINDLE

I decided to give the KDP Publishing Experience ago after seeing that so many people had enjoyed such success with this publishing platform. I had already written quite a few short stories so it made perfect sense to upload these onto the Kindle publishing platform.

From the beginning I found the Kindle platform to be intuitive and very easy to use. I was both surprised and relieved. Uploading my short stories was a breeze because the Kindle platform automatically converts your document file (in my case a word doc) and then converts it into the Kindle format.

Uploading your cover page for your eBook is also easy, I found it a breeze and I felt so proud when it was displayed in the Amazon bookstore. I write short stories so for me Kindle is a gift and is perfect for other writers to showcase their literary offering to the world.

Anything which I was unsure of - was pretty much covered on the Amazon site. I did have something which needed to be clarified and they came back to me - via email more or less straightaway. For Kindle it is imperative that you list your book in the right categories and that you choose the right keywords. There are thousands of books out there and you want to get them seen - right?

I made a blunder the first time around with my keywords. I found that they were too general, when I choose more specific keywords then I found that my books were more visible. The title of your book has to be accurate. To be honest the snappier the better, so I would suggest that you spend time on choosing the best title you can. I myself spend a considerable amount of time choosing a title because let's face it - you only get one chance to make a first impression.

Your description for your book has to convey all the relevant information without giving too much away, especially if your book is fictional. However what both you want to achieve whether your book is fiction or non-fiction - is reader curiosity. You want all of your potential readers to have an appetite for your book. You want them to buy your book at the end of the day!

People either buy your book because they want to be entertained or they want information - if you fail to deliver on both counts you could be may never take off!

If you are considering whether or not to go for it then I would give you a resounding Yes - it's fun!

Every day thousands of people worldwide are discovering the benefits of reading instant downloadable eBooks on their Amazon kindle, iPad, iPhone, or their computer. It offers an easy convenient way to read a book these days. Add that growing trend of e-readers to the already hugely popular Amazon, and you have one huge reason to publish on kindle.

Whether you are a marketer, non-fiction writer, or a fiction writer, publishing your book through kindle direct publishing can help you get your name out, your information out, and get your story out in a way that you have never been able to do before!

Publishing on kindle also helps you to gain credibility. You become an author when you publish on kindle. Having the word 'author' in front of your name instantly makes you an expert in the field you are writing about to readers.

All it takes is one successful kindle book to massively increase your credibility online, and in turn, increase your sales in other places both online and offline. One book can get the ball rolling for the rest of your career.

Thousands of people are now focusing their efforts towards kindle and earning a second income from it. Portions of those people are making full-time incomes through their kindle books. And other people are being discovered by movie producers and publishing companies on kindle, and they are being offered huge deals that promise massive future success.

How To Publish On Kindle

Kindle direct publishing makes it stress-free for you to get your book up and read for the world to see. Signing up to publish is a short process, and once you upload your book and cover, and fill in your price preferences, you can have your book live on Amazon in about twelve hours!

You don't even have to write the book yourself. If you have full rights to a book that someone else (ghostwriter) wrote, then you can attach your name to it and sell it for whatever price you want.

What You Need To Know

Even though it is easy to publish on kindle once you have a book created, there are many things that you need to know in order to find success with your book.

For instance, you need to know how to format your book so it transfers well to kindle, what kind of cover you should use, what price point sells best for your niche, and how to market your book after you publish it.

All of this information is important because in order to sell your book, you need to capture the interest of the reader. Just because a reader can see that it's for sale doesn't mean they are going to buy it.

Even though people shouldn't judge a book by its cover, they do. You can have the best information in the world inside the book, but if you can't catch the eye of your reader and draw them into your book through your cover, title, and price, then they will never read the inside.

The best way to learn how to be successful with kindle publishing is to follow the advice of someone who has had success. They have through with the testing and spent the money to learn what works and what doesn't, and by using their methods, you can save yourself a lot of time and headache. You don't need to re-invent the wheel to find success; you just need to find a process that works.

In the end, if you are an internet marketer or writer, or even just a normal guy or gal, you need to start thinking about how you can publish on kindle. It is one of the easiest ways to get your books published, gain a second income and it can help you gain a huge amount of credibility.

And when sales start to roll in for your eBook, you will be hooked and never look back!

-EBOOK SALES THROUGH AMAZON KINDLE PLATFORM

Kindle self-publishing has provided e-book authors fresh chances to make cash. Amazon's ebook reader device is considered the most favored one, meaning that the Kindle ebook publishing choice is very worthwhile.

Various uncomplicated tactics can help you make money with Kindle self-publishing. You can depend on various primary ideas to raise the popularity of your publications and to maximize income.

To generate income through Amazon kindle self-publishing, you will first have to put a excellent ebook together. People who are interested in ebook products have got a huge number of options to choose amongst. A well-written, properly designed publication is usually the only chance to jump out.

Discuss the topics you already know along with the things that you care about. Your abilities will become apparent in the very first pages of the ebook. Refrain from beginning an incredibly ambitious project that you're new to, even if you suspect that the area possesses significant money making possibilities.

Last but not least, for effective Kindle self-publishing, you'll need to depend upon skilled editing. There is absolutely no alternative, if you want to turn ebook publishing into a rewarding business enterprise.

Kindle Self-Publishing: A Picture Is Worth A 1000 Words!

You have a matter of moments to impress Amazon buyers. A fantastic book cover plus a intelligently written outline will allow you to be noticed. Here is your one possibility to seize the attention of the audience and to bring in revenue.

Expert, appealing and appropriate cover designs are the initial thing sellers observe. Lots of people make buying choices based on pictures. Developing a cover on your own is good, so long as you have got picture editing expertise. Utilizing top quality photos and interesting typefaces can help you put a stylish cover together.

The write-up on the eBook should really emphasize your main points. Including a handful of lines of positive reviews will establish some credibility and also increase the willingness of folks to buy.

Drive Traffic towards Your Kindle Self-Publishing Book Web page

To generate money using Kindle publishing, you'll have to do a lot of promoting. Internet supplies exceptional, free of charge publicity prospects. Depend upon those to get targeted traffic to your Amazon electronic book description pages.

Social networking is one of the techniques to master. Start a website or a blog and dedicate it to the topics discussed in your eBooks. Include a link to your Amazon URL in your e-mail signature and on your business card. All marketing opportunities should be utilized cleverly and efficiently to bring up sales and increase your Kindle book publishing success.

A number of the most effective Amazon eBook writers produce a small fortune through their work. The building of practical sales is achievable by everybody. You'll need a great idea in addition to a brilliant marketing and advertising strategy. A bit of time on the preliminary steps will let you create an intriguing eBook which has a substantial income creation possibilities.

-THE AMAZON KINDLE PLATFORM IS FOR BOTH WRITERS AND MARKETERS

Suppose you have a business or want to advance quickly in your career, the number one best thing you can do is establish yourself as an expert. You might think that expert status is something others confer on you, but it's very largely something that you do yourself! No one can agree that you're an expert if you don't keep up on the latest news and put your opinions out there. And there's no better way than with a book!

In the past, it was all but impossible to get a book published. Any writer knows that the process of getting the words down can take years -- but that's not all. Most writers also need an agent, even for nonfiction. That process can take six months to a year -- in some cases, far more. Once you have an agent, they have to "shop" the book to publishers. The big publishing houses often don't accept "simultaneous submissions," which means you have to wait for each rejection one at a time. They can each take years!

It's a wonder how any books got published at all under this system, right? Well, now there's an alternative. One can publish just about any book on the Amazon Kindle platform and make it available to millions of Kindle users as well as millions more who can view your book on other electronic platforms.

Kindle Publishing versus Vanity Publishing

One of the biggest scams to hit any industry in the last decade has been the explosive rise of vanity publishing. In vanity publishing, you submit your manuscript to a shady operation that publishes it after you pay them a fee. You might get a few copies and might be able to sell a few dozen to friends and family, but in the end you're left with nothing tangible and the "publisher" has taken you for a ride. Don't do it!

By contrast, publishing on Kindle lets you maintain control over your work. You will still have to provide proofreading, copy editing, and other services -- but the truth is that vanity publishers don't provide these, anyway. You will also have to get someone to make a compelling, "book-like" cover if you want your offerings to stand out in the crowd. But beyond that, Kindle publishing is free and you get royalties per sale.

Why Kindle Publishing Beats Traditional Publishing Hands Down

When you go to a bookstore, it's obvious which authors the store "wants" you to choose. The ones who get the big storefront displays are considered sure bets by management and the corporate office. Those on the back shelves can expect to be "remaindered off" in a hurry -- in other words, if the store orders ten copies of a book and only sells two in a few weeks, they might only order two during the next sales cycle.

That means that, as coveted as a position on the bookstore shelves is, it's a losing proposition for most authors. For all their big talk, publishing houses don't generally spend much money promoting new authors. It's up to the author to do as much of the promotion as possible and, if they are favored, to write another book as quickly as possible so it, too, can be remaindered off. Success is the exception, not the rule.

In most cases, you'll have a fighting chance as a Kindle publisher that you won't get as an author newly in print from a big publishing house. That's because people will be able to discover your book when they do their ordinary, everyday Amazon searches. It's even easier for a new author to get attention from a reader who is shopping on the Kindle.

When you buy books in the Kindle Store, there is virtually no distinction made between establishment authors and newcomers. Your works could appear alongside the most trusted authorities in your field. Plus, there are fewer expectations when it comes to the length of your book. Most customers are happy to pay for a 50-page work that answers their questions effectively and gives them value, versus a 200-page work by a multi-time author that's full of hot air -- intended to meet publishing house guidelines for size.

Naturally, when you publish on the Kindle, you should enlist help. Get a proofreader to help you make sure that your copy (that is, the words in your piece) meets up to the standards of the big publishing houses. Find someone who can make you an eye-catching "cover," since that will be a huge factor in driving sales -- nobody wants to buy a Kindle book that doesn't have the same look and feel of a real book. If users are disappointed, bad reviews will drag down your sales.

But also try to worry less and enjoy the process. You have creative control!

-How To Get Published In Amazon Kindle Platform

Publish a book - Amazon Kindle is the latest fad in online sales, and everybody's doing it. Why isn't you? Maybe you've ended up being sidetracked or simply detoured by what you really feel to be an absence of "technical expertise", yet rest assured, anyone could release their very own e-book via Kindle self-publishing by merely writing their e-book, creating a cover image, and picking a royalty alternative. It's simply that simple. Don't think me? Keep reading.

Keys To Creating Your E-book

For several, writing the eBook itself may be the most daunting difficulty, but once it's finished, everything else is a breeze. When writing your eBook, keep in mind that your e-book must be formatted appropriately in order to be approved by Amazon. Amazon Kindle eReader does permit most DOC declare digital publication sale, nonetheless, utilizing a standard word processing program such as Microsoft Word or Open office is advised.

Amazon Kindle eReader permits most DOC files to be utilized for digital manual sale, nonetheless, doctor documents that have challenging formatting could not operate properly or could merely fail to upload entirely. So if at all possible, attempt to make use of. Doctor data such as Word files or Open workplace doctors rather than. docx or transportable file data. Using bold and italic formatting within your e-book is high quality, yet anything beyond that, which is a lot more intricate, such as bullet points, is just not suitable with the Amazon Kindle eReader. Are you acquainted with the stating, "A photo's well worth a thousand words"? Photo within your e-book are a must. Just make certain that you really own the copyright, obviously. All images need to be made use of as. jpg documents, and centered. However, if you attempt to cover photos around content, it may look good on your personal PC display, yet considering as your material will be viewed on mobile tools, it will certainly look totally different to your audiences. So when formatting your eBook, please keep these tips in mind.

After you have actually obtained the writing of your e-book made good, it's time to make some catchy heading title pages, and also acknowledgment pages. If you want, you could insert a web page break anywhere within your e-book that you feel a tough page break should be, and it will of course program within the final of your Amazon Kindle e-book. Numerous of you may discover the technical aspects of word-processing tough or taxing, and in this situation, it's much better to just outsource this part of the e-book creation to a certified professional that can help you get the "look and feel" you prefer.

As soon as you have actually got the "look and feel" you prefer, simply transform it to among the approved Amazon Kindle styles stated above, then it's "off" to make the most coveted part of your e-book: the cover.

Innovative E-book Cover Styles

In this business first impressions count. You have actually just obtained round to "catch the eye" of your visitors, so you much better make it count! Many e-book developers merely fall short to put in the time needed to create high-quality e-book covers, and it reveals not just via the visuals, but much more significantly from their lack of sales. There are thousands of various other e-books on Amazon, so make sure to make your "title" and "picture" pop. All set to obtain paid? Let's talk aristocracies...

Getting Paid & Royalties

OK. Worrying royalty alternatives, you've got 2 selections: 35 % or 70 %, minus shipping fees. In order to decide on the 70 % royalty choice, your eBook needs to fall within the $2.99 and $9.99 rate range. Your e-book has to additionally not include any public domain info and have a Kindle selling price equal to or less than the market price of any type of hardback/physical manual currently readily available within your very same specific niche. By making these demands, Amazon makes certain that e-books aren't overpriced and do not cost more than normal hardback books would. That makes good sense right? Obviously it does.

Well, now you know the essential parts to offer your first Amazon Kindle e-book efficiently. Exactly what are you waiting? Amazon Kindle is the latest trend in online sales, and everyone's doing it ... Now you can as well! Anyone could release their own e-book with Kindle self-publishing by just composing their manual, producing a cover image, and selecting an aristocracy option. It's just that simple!

Hello Abigail has published a book on amazon and has an experience on how to be successful on amazon. By creating a book and publishing it on amazon you can actually make real good income on amazon if you know what you are doing. do check out the URL include on book publishing. good luck.

-AMAZING TIPS THAT WILL SURELY MAKE YOU A LOT OF MONEY ONLINE PUBLISHING EBOOKS ON KINDLE

Getting Started

Ok I know what's going through your mind - "I can't write, I don't know where to start, what do I do etc" Ok now don't panic because I'm going to show you a really easy and cheap way to get your own content that's totally original.

Here's How Easy It Can Be

One easy way around writing it is to use PLR. But if you're going to do that, make sure you make it totally original. There was a news article about some marketer supposedly telling people to slap together eBooks with PLR and this led to a huge crackdown by Amazon. They basically have a no-PLR rule.

You can still use PLR, but take the time to change it and make it original. You really should do this anyway. How would you feel if you bought a book and it turned out to be the same as another one you'd bought, just with a different cover?

Another option is to use public domain. There are lots of public domain materials available that you can repackage and sell as your own. Since these are already out there, you have to make it different somehow. You can add a commentary or put several public domain texts into one new collection.

Tips on Making A Killing With Kindle

First of all, quality really matters with Kindle. People are actually reading these books and if you give them crap, they'll refund it. Lots of Internet marketers have found this out the hard way. You should also be aware that eventually Amazon will erase your books if they don't meet their quality standards. Publishing on Kindle is a long-term strategy, not something that's get-rich-quick.

When you're thinking of topics, you should pick something general in your niche. This guarantees that people will start buying it. Topics that are too obscure usually don't sell so well.

Be Realistic

Now, you're not going to make a whole ton of money from one book. The best strategy is to start your own publishing empire. Pump those titles onto Kindle and then track the results. People who make lots of money do so because they have lots of titles.

You can also use your Kindle books for lead generation. Somewhere in your book, put a link to your site or the affiliate sites you're promoting. You can also offer special coupons in the book that they can use for your services.

Kindle is really hot now and it's far from saturated. Lots of marketers aren't getting with the program, so it'll really benefit you if you do. That's it for Kindle. Get some books published and see for yourself how powerful this tool is.

-GENERAL FORMATTING GUIDELINES FOR CREATING A KINDLE EBOOK

It is widely known that Amazon Kindle has opened the gates for all types of authors, published and unpublished, to effortlessly broadcast a new book and establish an audience of loyal followers. An imperative aspect that many tend to overlook is formatting books in a user-friendly, aesthetically pleasing, and exciting way to capture a good portion of the millions of potential viewers Kindle offers. Formatting is the key to producing an eBook that is both profitable and successful online.

Your First 10% Will Make-It or Break-It

When utilizing the Kindle platform the first ten percent of your eBook is offered as a costless taster to allow readers to wet their lips with your content. If they detect value in your writing they will buy it. If not, they simply won't. The idea here is to give your reader content they can put a price on. Do not put your Title Page and Table of Contents right at the beginning, which I know is contradictory to what many formatting guides recommend. Having these two aspects as the only things your potential buyers can view makes it too easy for them to make a quick judgment based off of looks and content headers. You want to be sure readers are hooked on your writing ability and intend to buy your eBook, not hope that one of your headings may catch their eye and intrigue them enough to end in a purchase.

Break away from the norm and entice your reader with a tantalizing introduction. Familiarize them with your individual writing style by providing a synopsis of the fantasy journey you'll be leading them on or sell them on the concept that you withhold the necessary solution to their current issue.

Spicy Colors Supplemented With Lively Images

Pages upon pages of boring black text is a sure fire way to turn what was a feeling of excitement into complete boredom. Humans don't see the world in black and white so why make your readers? Strive to bring your words to life with vibrate colors and images. Nurture a connection between text and imagery. These elegant text breakers will aid readers in formulating a link between the points you are making and how they relate to the world we live in.

Aesthetically Pleasing Organization

Create an organized structure by implementing headings and subheadings by grouping relevant topics that share similar points of interests into a common section. Tell your reader what they can expect from a particular segment. While your eBook is centralized on one core topic your reader may only show interest in a particular subtopic at the moment.

Provide accessibility of finding that subtopic by clearly cataloging where it rests within your entire work. Let your heading and subheadings stand out with Bolding, Italicizing, and Underlining. You want topics to jump off the page and attract reader's eyes with importance.

White Space intertwined suitably within a body of work can deliver much more than just blank space, it permits your reader a moment to rest their eyes. Utilize this tactic when you are explaining large topics so readers feel more accomplished when they master each individual section.

All of these concepts can be simply utilized by viewing your own eBook from the outside perspective of your buyer. Do not think about how changing a particular aspect is going to affect your time and publication date as a writer. Think about what eases your buyer's reading experience and the value they receive from your work. Remember formatting books is all about captivating with the first ten percent by grasping prospects with an intriguing introduction, allowing for content breaking colors supplemented with related images, and wrapping your book together in an aesthetically pleasing package.

-TABLE GUIDELINES FOR CREATING A KINDLE EBOOK

The Amazon Kindle, and the Kindle Direct Publishing (KDP) platform, has created tremendous opportunities for writers to publish their work. Instead of wasting years trying to get the attention of a major publishing house, they can sell their work directly through the Kindle store. But, there is still an obstacle in the way of success - formatting.

Bad formatting of your Kindle eBook is nearly guaranteed to generate negative reviews from readers and formatting problems can easily sneak into your eBook. Unlike publishing PDF eBooks, what you see in your word processor is not necessarily what you will get when you upload your book to the KDP system. There are also a few invisible formatting steps that will make your eBook work like Kindle readers expect it to perform.

To get you moving on the track of Kindle publishing success, here is a short list of best practices for formatting your eBook for the Amazon Kindle:

Remove Document Headers and Footers

Include a Clickable Table of Contents

Bookmark the Table of Contents and First Page

Use Formatting Styles in your Word Processor

Start Chapters on a New Page

Avoid "Special" Formatting

Always Proof Read before Publishing

Remove Document Headers and Footers

The Kindle format does not allow headers and footers in an eBook. If you have them in the document you upload for publication the best case scenario is that they will be stripped out. The worst case is that they will cause massive formatting issues for your eBook. The easiest solution is to simply turn them off. The same goes for page numbering. Turn them off.

Include a Clickable Table of Contents

Readers appreciate a table of contents on any book long enough to contain multiple chapters. The exception is works of fiction. Many Kindle devices, like the Kindle Fire, have touch screens. Making your table of contents entries clickable allows readers to easily navigate around your eBook and access the content they are most interested in reading.

When adding a table of contents do not include page numbers and restrict entries to chapters. Pages are a fluid concept in Kindle eBook and will change based on the font size users select and the screen size of the device. Limiting the entries to chapters only will keep your table of contents from getting cluttered.

Bookmark the Table of Contents and First Page

Kindle readers and Kindle software apps allow readers to jump to the cover, the table of contents, and the beginning of the content. Those spots in your eBook are identified using bookmarks. The KDP platform will add the cover bookmark when they convert your eBook for publication and add the cover graphic you provide. Add a bookmark labeled "TOC" just before your table of contents and another labeled "Start" just before the title of your first chapter. Then the KDP system will know where to send readers when they navigate through your eBook.

Use Formatting Styles in your Word Processor

Microsoft Word, Open Office, and other modern word processors allow you to control the look of your document using styles. If you are not using styles to format your documents, start now. Instead of manually adjusting the font styles, sizes, and other attributes one-by-one through the whole document, styles let you make changes to the whole document in one place.

Chapter titles should always be labeled as "Heading 1". The Kindle publishing system will automatically detect the text labeled as "Heading 1" and identify it as a new chapter. Readers will be able to jump through your eBook chapter-by-chapter and you will be able to use your word processor's automatic table of contents tools as well.

Start Chapters on a New Page

Add a page break before each chapter. This helps to create a clear separation between chapters and readers expect it. You can add this page break using the style settings. Just edit the "Heading 1" style and select "add page break before." Your document will automatically update itself and add a page break before every chapter title (see how handy those styles are?)

Avoid "Special" Formatting

The Kindle eBook format is very minimalist to ensure a good user experience across a wide range of devices. Special characters, bullets, special fonts, tabs, and tables do not translate well. Stick to the basics like bold, italics, indents, and underlines for consistent results.

Always Proof Read before Publishing

Even if you follow every best practice when formatting your eBook, errors can (and do) creep in during the conversion process. Amazon provides a preview tool for publishers to review a converted eBook before publishing. You can also download a copy of the converted eBook to your own Kindle device or one of the many Kindle apps available. Review your entire eBook. Look for strange formatting. Click every link in your table of contents and make sure it goes to the right spot. Use the navigation tools to jump around your eBook and make sure they take you to the right spots.

Fix problems in your main document, upload the new version to the KDP system and review the revised files. Repeat the process until you find no more problems. Then, you are ready to publish your eBook and share it with the world.

If you keep an eye on these best practices, you will create an eBook that functions the way Kindle owners expect it to work. Then, they will be focused on the content of your words and not distracted by formatting errors. With a little time and effort, your book can look every bit as professional as the latest blockbuster from the big New York publishing houses.

-ASSET GUIDELINES FOR CREATING A KINDLE EBOOK

Authors and poets are very inspiring and incredible part of our society. These people are popular due to their magical words that can make anyone fall in love. Because of their popularity sometimes, the edition of their books in market gets scared. Fans have to wait a lot for new edition. In order to cope up with this issue, publishing books on internet has become fashion. It is extremely easy, even for novice, to get their books publish on any website. This substitute process of publishing books spare them from hectic wait and wastage of money. They can conveniently produce as many copies as they want without wasting money and putting excessive efforts. However, the only important thing for publishing a book on internet is to write a quality material. For this purpose, there are some important tips that can help one write a perfect e-book. Some of these tips are as follow:

Important Tips:

Below given tips are extremely essential for jotting down an effective e-book.

Topic:

First, it is imperative to be sure about topic of book one is planning to write. Every aspect of that subject should be clear and competently in grip of the writer. For instance, if a person is going to write about different languages, he/she must have complete expertise on this subject.

Target audience:

In order to write an impressive book, it is imperative to consider whom you are writing for. Furthermore, evaluate the question that what necessary information one is going to deliver. Besides, it is very vital to know who your target audience is. All of these questions will help one to be more attentive and narrow towards his topic.

Focus:

In order to deliver a quality work, one needs to be very specific on his/her topic. It is essential to remain focus on subject. Try not to include inappropriate details and data. It will give a poor impact of your work. If one is a novice then it is very essential to build an impressive image that can catch attention of maximum audience.

Add Summary:

It is extremely important to add a summary of your article or book at end. On internet, people do not go through complete article. Rather, they just skim through the article. In order to give a reader complete knowledge of article or book, it is imperative to add summary at the end. This point is extremely important to enhance the quality of your e-book.

CHAPTER 3

SELLING ITEMS ON AMAZON

-HOW TO EARN MONEY IN THE AMAZON SELLING PLATFORM

Okay, so now you want to make money on the internet. So what made you try the technique? Have you lately learned from somebody that the internet is an amazing way of making some quick money? Or perhaps you may have visited some website which promises to make you millionaire overnight just by doing some basic work? Well, if these are the cases, let me warn you, the thing is not that simple. It takes days of dedication and hard work to make a fortune online, but yes, of course it is totally possible to make a full-time income from the comfort of your home with nothing but a PC and an internet connection.

In this article, we will discuss 5 steps that can be taken to instantly start a profitable business from home. We will be talking about Affiliate Marketing. It is a very beginner-friendly method of making some money, and hence we will make this guide as step-by-step as possible.

Step 1

Go to ClickBank.com or Amazon.com and signup for a free account. These are the most popular affiliate websites where you will get paid if someone buys a product using your affiliate link. The commission depends on a variety of factors, but ClickBank.com generally pays a lot more than what Amazon does, but again, Amazon has a lot more products to choose from, and is a lot more reputed site.

Step 2

The next step is to select a good product to promote. If you select ClickBank go to your account and sort the items in order of their gravity, or payout commission amount, the one you prefer. If on Amazon, you will have to select the bestsellers, or the hottest items of the moment, and make an appropriate selection.

Step 3

Next step is to build a website or a blog around the product, the site that you are going to use to promote it to people and earn commissions. You can signup for a cheap website from GoDaddy, or if you do not wish to spend any money, you ca build a blog with blogger.com or WordPress.com. Then you have to write some content for the site/blog using the descriptions or reviews that you find elsewhere, most commonly in the product description page of ClickBank or Amazon itself. Make it sound like you are a neutral buyer, and just suggesting others to try it. The sad reality is no one lover internet marketers!

Step 4

In this step all you want to do is get your site indexed with Google. The most primary thing that you can do is to go to the various bookmarking site, and bookmark your pages. Also, do not forget to ping your site with a site called pingomatic.com. In this way, you will succeed in getting the attention of Google, and get indexed so that others find your site when they are looking for the product.

Step 5

Go and promote your site everywhere! Post a video on YouTube, make blog posts with other Web 2.0 properties, and indulge in discussions in other related forums. Do whatever it takes to bring traffic to your site, because it is the traffic that will determine the amount of money that you will earn from the internet.

-THINGS YOU NEED TO GET STARTED IN SELLING ITEMS IN THE AMAZON SELLING PLATFORM

Amazon.com was one of the first affiliate programs which allowed you to sell books online. They are still one of the largest online retailers in the world and have an excellent affiliate program.

Today you can also make money as an affiliate doing things such as getting leads or getting people to click on ads. Google Adsense is an example of this.

Now let's look at the 3 simple affiliate marketing steps.

1. **Choose a niche**. Find something that you have an interest in or are passionate about.

This is good advice because you will stick with it even when you're not making money at first. It might also be something that you have knowledge on and could turn into an Internet business.

One of the tricks to making money with affiliate marketing is to brand yourself as an expert in the niche you choose. Being passionate about it, or knowledgeable on it, will help you do that.

2. **Find affiliate programs**. Most affiliate programs are free to join.

Merchants are looking for people to represent their products online. Finding products or programs is not hard to do. Joining and affiliate network is a good way to get started.

Google Adsense is the top pay per click affiliate program. Commission Junction is the top cost per action affiliate program..

ClickBank is the largest digital information affiliate program. Amazon is a great program to find physical products to sell.

If you join these 4 you will have plenty products to promote online. You might want to start with Google Adsense and then branch out from there.

3. **Promote like crazy**. You can promote the affiliate marketing website when you first get started.

Some people will start a free blog at Blogger.com which is owned by Google. This is also a fast way to get approved for the Google Adsense affiliate program.

Eventually you may want to become more professional and host your own blog. There are many quality hosting companies such as Blue Host and Host Gator you can join.

This will involve purchasing your own domain names. Godaddy and Name Cheap are 2 good places to do that.

Use the Fantastico program that your hosting company will provide. This is a fast way to set up a WordPress blog which is the number one blogging platform in the world today.

One of the things that is good about simple affiliate marketing is it doesn't take any technical knowledge to get started. This is true whether you host your own blog or just promote your affiliate website directly.

CHAPTER 4

FREELANCING

-THINGS YOU NEED TO TAKE INTO CONSIDERATION BEFORE DELVING IN THE WORLD OF

FREELANCING

Freelancers are self-employed individuals who specialize in a particular field. People who go into freelancing have often built up a large repertoire of skills through agency and business employment. The demand for their skills is often high however the individual is able to earn potentially more through freelancing.

Functioning as a freelancer is an attractive prospect to many as it allows people to potentially earn more and work to their own schedule. This seems great however there are many challenges and things to consider before becoming a freelancer.

Time

Many people fall into the trap of believing that they will have more time when freelancing. This is often not the case because you have to do many of the tasks that you wouldn't have to do when working for a business. These include administration and accounting. When working for a business you also have a set time in which you are expected to work. With freelancing you have to work whatever hours it takes to complete a job.

One of the major challenges freelancers face is time management. It can become difficult for them to separate personal and work time. If you are good at this then you might be able to reduce the overall hours that you work.

Working Alone

It can come as quite a shock to many who are new to freelancing as they are used to the bustle of lively office. If you like having people around you then freelancing might not be for you. The benefit of working alone is the ability to have the quiet surroundings in order to concentrate. It really depends on personal preference.

One of the big drawbacks of freelancing can be having no one there to bounce ideas off. If you thrive on this then you might find freelancing a bit slow. At present most freelancers will use Twitter to source thoughts on ideas.

Focus and Discipline

If you are a focused individual who is driven and able to set themselves target then freelancing would be a good option. People who are distracted easily and find it difficult to focus might struggle with freelancing. This is because when at home there are many things to distract you. In a work environment you are expected to work and behave in a certain way. With some people it can take a little bit of time to get used to this.

Generating Sales

This is crucial. If you are not able to generate sales then you will not be able to sustain your living. Time has to be set aside to generate sales and in slow periods you might have to find alternative sources of income. In some industries it is easier to do this than others. It is often advised to have a few clients on board before you move full time into freelancing.

These are some of the things you should consider. If you think you have these qualities then you could benefit hugely.

-A STEP BY STEP GUIDE IN CREATING A FREELANCE PROFILE

For those who are fascinated by making extra cash with freelancing and beginning a job in the field of blogging, starting a blog with blogger.com is considered the first step. To do so, visit the blogger.com front page and commence planning what you will do with all the money when it starts to roll in!

The homepage of blogger.com shows a vibrant colored and directional box which explains a few of the simple measures towards developing a blog, which has an orange colored arrow directing you what to do to begin with. Then click on that arrow and your process begins. The page requests for your email address, then to retype the email address. This is the email address which you'll use to log on on your blog on blogger.com in virtually any future trips to your site.

Next you must pick out a password around the parameters of your requirements of blogger.com, with a view to safely make easy money. Whilst you type possible password selections, underneath you're going to be told whether or not the strength of the password is high or low, that allows you to decide on a password that is at least eight characters with the best security. After this you should retype the password thereafter set up a display name.

Afterward you read and accept the terms of use and commence the next measure. If, however, you may have a Google account created, you'll be able to skip this step and move straight away to the "sign in to Blogger using your Google Account" section, and input your email and password. Once these easy steps are completed then you can begin earning extra income through freelancing.

Once this has been completed, the next phase in starting your blog using blogger.com requires you to name your brand-new venture and being making easy money with freelancing. You enter a title for the blog, then you select an address in your blog. This acts as the method in which you and also other people can link your web blog to many other sites. The url is what precedes ".blogspot.com". You could prefer to host your blog site someplace else which has an advanced blog constructed and therefore increase your opportunity to make easy money. After that step, you are able to opt for the template that you want with regards to your personalized blog.

While you execute this, you are able to change the template you choose at a later time, or perhaps you can modify the blog template. Right now, your blog has been activated. It is live and now you can start adding posts, creating and updating your own profile, and taking advantage of the blog tools to customize your site.

Right now you are ready to start out writing the first blog and making easy money with freelancing. Under the "posting" tab in the top left, select "create" below it after which when you have put a title, you may compose the first section of online writing, which may include editing the format, font, size, placement, adding pictures and creating attachments. Once you've finished composing your website one can publish it right then or save it for a future time. That is everything you need to be able to begin a blog with blogger.com and earn easy money with freelancing.

-A Step By Step Guide On Selection Of Jobs And Compensation

Businesses worldwide are looking for individuals to do a variety of freelance professional services from remote locations. The outsourcing of business operations is the right thing to do for businesses that cannot afford to hire another employee, yet have needs beyond those their current employees can fulfill.

Those subcontractors who operate online can work from the comfort of their own home, or small office if they have one, and can find clients from across the world. Most of the work subcontracted via job auction websites are one-time tasks, for example the writing of a report or the programming of an application.

Still, these sites provide the ability for freelance business services providers to establish their own profile and sustain a web presence by giving them a personal space on their website. Such a system makes it feasible to build more work from previous clients and work towards securing full-time subcontracting work. For the best chance at a quick start, lots of freelancers use one of the following established, respected websites: oDesk; Elance; Get A Freelancer.

Working through an online auction website, freelance service providers are solely responsible for their professional reputation. Clients can leave feedback and ratings on the profile of the provider. Providers must be able to keep their own books, sell their own services, seek out their own online opportunities, and manage their own scheduling and deadlines. No one is going to assist and finish the project in the case of the provider having an emergency.

People thinking of joining any job auction websites, should note the below steps to maximize their likelihood of succeeding:

- Read all help tutorials to learn the rules, etiquette and processes of the site.
- Spend a couple of days a week looking through job postings to ascertain if the sorts of project you're interested in is on the market and whether your experience qualify you for it.
- Take the time to construct a solid profile. An empty profile is a sign to others that a freelancer isn't serious about finding work.
- Visit freelancing blogs and forums, to learn more about the site.
- Produce an online portfolio of samples of whatever type of work you do. Refer prospective employers to your online portfolio, or attach samples to bids.
- Make a standard contract or use a sample work order from the job auction website.

-EMPLOYER AND/OR CLIENT FEEDBACK IS CRUCIAL TO YOUR SUCCESS AS A FREELANCER

Hiring a great freelance programmer for your programming project isn't as difficult as it may sound. Have no doubts that you simply can discover most likely more programmers who can do your job and do it well. You will find a couple of essential dos and don'ts if you would like to hire the proper coder for your job. There's a very general process you'll wish to usually follow when embarking on such an endeavor. The following write-up explains a few key factors that you have to look out for

You have a lot of responsibility here because initial of all your project description must be crystal clear so there's 100% understanding. You can't anticipate them to know everything on their own since they're programmers and not marketers. They'll only go from the description and anything else you have written, so make sure that there are plenty of details for them to follow. It's frustrating for you in the event you receive the end result and something isn't working precisely like you planned. Clear and frequent communications, when necessary, are the key to obtaining the project carried out correctly and on time. If you want to give the project the very best chance of succeeding, then don't neglect open and clear communications. You have to give your feedback on his approach and everything else so that you are able to get the most out of it. There's a time and place for everything, so steer clear of sending a dozen emails each day to the individual you hire. Any project is a concerted effort by all to ensure success which is of course the goal for everybody involved. What you would like to do as soon as function begins is continue to develop a positive working relationship. Every great programmer expects to share a powerful relationship with their client, so always keep this in mind.

It is crucial that you make certain any paperwork is produced and agreed upon between you and your freelance programmer. That's just the very essential administrative job, and it'll also permit everybody to feel they are able to proceed with concern. This also keeps things clear within the long run, to ensure that the project doesn't need to suffer because of unknown circumstances. When you begin your hunting procedure, you'll come across numerous programmers that claim to be the very best in their field, but unless and until you scrutinize them, don't commit. These are just a few of the steps you should take before hiring any type of freelance employee. This write-up is by no means comprehensive, so continue your education regarding the task of hiring a freelancer.

CHAPTER 5

BLOGGING

-BENEFITS OF BLOGGING TO EARN MONEY ONLINE

We all want to know the technical stuff about how to build a successful blog 'cash machine'.

But it's knowing WHY you want or need to do it that will carry you through the 'leveling off' phases where you are wondering what to do next. You need to have a good reason; a gut reason to do what has to be done to get through the learning curve.

So here I'm going to give you 9 good reasons to build your own money making blog. Take your pick!

1) Retirement plan

Many seniors are wondering when they will be able to retire with some money in their pockets. Will I be able to keep my job 'til 65? Will I have to work until 72 years old to get a full pension? I just don't feel like working like a dog anymore. I just can't keep up.

First of all who says you have to work until you are 65 years old? It's not a matter of age but having enough money coming in to retire.

You are maybe older (I'm 61 in 2014) but you can make money from the experience you have acquired. Learn how to write a book to publish on Amazon, a video training series or email courses. There are people who are smart enough to invest a bit of money and gain years of learning time by using other people's know-how.

There are thousands of bloggers who have multiple streams of income coming in. They do 'niche marketing' and offer through affiliate programs like that of Amazon, Commission Junction, Click Bank products that specific groups of people are interested in.

They make a good living and only work 10 to 15 hours a week.

Need to get to know these people, right?

Even if you are 5 years away from your goal, you start working towards it now because you can get your time investment back very quickly.

2) A woman's dream (you deserve it don't you?)

Most women have a financial disadvantage in the working world. They just don't make as much as the men for the same job. Well this is not at all true of the Internet blogging world.

Bloggers freely share their insights and knowledge and there isn't a competitive spirit. This seems to be closer to the woman's way of doing things.

Imagine being able to be a stay-at-home-mom, not losing a single moment of those precious moments with the children (and your lover too). But also being able to share something that you are passionate about: book reviews, container gardening, patchwork, couponing.

Imagine bringing in 2 to 3,000$ a month all the while investing only 10-15 hours a week of your time, would it be worth learning how?

Of course it would!

3) Upgrade your personal market value

You develop your professional competence by having a blog. And you stay in contact with the working world even if for a time you are unemployed or underemployed.

What can you learn by blogging?

How to manage and promote a Website

How to market a book or product

Better your writing skills. According to Reader's Digest your mastery of vocabulary is one of the decisive factors in getting high paying jobs.

Learning to get out of your 'comfort zone'

Develop a network of positive, active contacts that can coach you to success.

Learn how to set a goal and achieve it.

Do you think a boss would fire a person like you? He would be crazy not to keep (or hire) a positive, idea creating, goal setting person like you.

Hardly anyone will do what it takes to go to the end of a project if they don't know WHY they would sacrifice television time, fooling around time or sport's fans time. WHY make the mental effort to learn? The easy way out is to just coast along and make no waves. Why build my own money making blog?

4) Feeling fulfilled

You may be handicapped or have a long term sickness. Or you may be in a job situation where you are an engineer working as a janitor to make ends meet. You may be highly educated from another country but not means to express your talents.

Well with a blog you can express your vision and creativity before hundreds of people that visit your forum.

Whatever your handicap, it makes no difference on a blog.

5) You can create your business with very little means (No financial risk)

Hosting your site with Hostgator.com costs 12$ a year. Choosing a domain name on namecheap.com around 12£ also. Word Press is free. And an autoresponder account like A weber is 19$ a month.

The real investment is the time you need to get yourself trained. But you do that at home from your computer.

But probably if you had to buy a franchise with a 100K to 1000K investment and that you lose it all (by contract) if you don't follow very precisely every single step with at least a 12 hour day time commitment, you would be more driven to succeed.

Eight people out of ten fail in their business in the first five years and often lose their shirt.

You may not make much money for a while until you get through the learning curve. But you can't lose your shirt by blogging.

But if you work at this like a business you can expect business-like revenues in the near future.

If you do what others don't want to do, you will have in 2 years' time (the time and money) which others still don't have. It only takes 1 year on internet to become an expert in a given area. An Expert is someone who knows more concerning a subject than 95% of the others.

6) You can become 'financially independent' even in times of crisis

Everyone knows you shouldn't have all your eggs in the same basket.

My father had the 'Dutch store' on the main street of a small town in Ontario. The town hall decided that the sewer system had to be redone and ripped out the whole street. Old people had to go over slippery board walks to get to the store. It was too much effort and they started to look for easier ways to get their groceries. Unexpectedly, the public works company who had probably put in a bid that was too low went under and was not able to finish the work. The situation stayed that way for two years. I don't know how my father survived this event but as a good Dutch immigrant he found the solutions by diversifying his income streams.

What does this have to do with a money making blog?

In times of crisis one product may no longer sell as well. Then you just find out what people are buying and do reviews on it on a new blog site you set up with links to the affiliate partner that sells it. Often 50-75% of the sales price is deposited on your account and they usually pay out the commissions every 15 days like clockwork.

Nothing stops you from having several blogs on different themes that you are passionate about.

Of course what sells very well in times of economic instability is any training in new ways of making money. And with Internet you can get trained by the best of the best marketers.

7) No geographical limitations

One of the best known experts in the survival field in France (where I live) who sells some 10,000 books on Amazon every month lives in...Montana.

With a blog you can live where you want. Being tied to a job location is no longer pertinent! That IS real freedom. How much do we do every day that we don't want to do but that we have to do to keep food on the table?

Do you want to spend some time (several months) in the French Alps? What about Marrakesh? Austria, Paris, Cancun?

What about doing some mission or humanitarian work for a time. You can write your articles for your blog from anywhere, can't you? Even on the beach.

What about having the time to visit with people that you love to be with?

We are in the middle of a paradigm shift (a new way of thinking and doing) that most of the world can't even dream about. And you have access to this!

8) Automatic sales and delivery procedures

There are many automatic sales process systems out there.

Did you know that once your sales letter has been written (with very few modifications) it can continue to bring in money for years to come?

Do you know that your FAQ's (frequently asked questions) can treat 95% of what your clients are asking?

And the software available allows you to get orders from most countries in the world 24/7. That beats having limited store hours and personnel problems doesn't it?

9) Your blog is worth money.

If you have a proven cash flow and your company is running on automatic, it's worth money! If you master the technical side of a money making blog and your financial statement shows profit, you can sell it for 10 times its average monthly cash flow. Let's say your blog is making 2,000$ average for the last two years, you could negotiate for a value of 20,000$ on flippa.com.

There are people who have more money than time to learn the stuff. For you, it's a way to monetize the time you spent to get there.

That said, if you can get to 2,000$ a month, it's probably just a matter of getting more traffic to get to 10,000$ per month. How many people using real estate to flip houses can say they are making that much without having to invest or take a risk or loss when the market crashes?

Consider your blog as a web property. If you've done it once you can do it again much faster.

This is like a life insurance for your family. In most physical businesses, if the key person disappears, or a fire destroys it or the market blows out, all is not lost if your business runs automatically.

This is a dream that you can make come true if you get started now!

But let's be clear about this: The distance between ignorance and knowledge is not as great as the distance between knowing what to do and just doing it!

-A STEP BY STEP GUIDE ON BUILDING YOUR BLOG

Why you have to choose to build a blog?

A blog is basically your own website that you can use for whatever purpose you like. To talk about current event or your favorite topics, or you can use it to market and promote stuff.

You may heard that sometimes Internet marketers call it niche marketing. It is all the same. More recently, people have been realizing the benefits of using their blogs to create an opt-in list.

The money truly is in the list, trust me! From a general quality list, you should be able to gain ROI as high as 1000% or more. And the ROI will continue increasing because when you have a better relationship with your list, you will be able to gain more.

All you have to do is set up your blog to have an email address form on it. Then, you write a short, informative report on the topic of your niche and offer it to your readers for FREE in exchange for their email address.

Simple, but it is so effective. Your readers (and future customers for life!) will type in their first name and email address into your auto-responder form (look up auto-responder if you are not familiar with what it is) in order to download your free report.

You'll harvest their email addresses, you have begun building your blog opt-in list!

Now you have so many opportunities to make money with your list once you have built a responsive one.

Remember, your list doesn't have to be huge in order to make you a recurring income that you can live very comfortably off of.

It is all about the relationship you create/build with your list and the quality of the material that you give them (and also sell them).

An opt-in list is a vital and valuable asset for any business, especially online ones.

A blog is just a great tool for you to use to build your list. It's free, it gets picked up easily by the search engines, it's a wide used platform that you can find additional functionality easily and it looks professional!

To be able to build a list for FREE that can earn you literally millions of dollars is quite an incredible phenomenon and we should all be grateful for this great opportunity.

-HOW TO CREATE A HIGH-QUALITY, INFORMATIVE, USEFUL AND VALUABLE CONTENT THAT YOUR VISITORS WILL LOVE

One of the more tough things to do while putting up a blog is to retain its freshness. If you desire to get enough traffic positively along with readers and fans, you need to ensure that your blog always offers something new along with something thrilling. Just delivering quality content will not be enough. You need to publish the content and the whole blog in a good and inspirational manner. In case the people go to see the blog find it to be boring, it's quite likely that they will not come back and possibly will not even read the rest of the blog. This will end to you losing readership and page views. All your hard work in building the good content will go to waste. So, how to keep your blog fresh? Te answer is simple: Put forth adequate commitment and try being creative.

Using commitment to the blog can cause great things to the blog as you make money on internet. Using commitment means giving sufficient time to read and study the best blog posts and even the blog content. You can read the top and the most recommended blogs and spot the reason for their success. Always concentrate on learning their way of presentation and how they attract readers. This will get you enough resources to decide what you need to do for your blog. You can browse through the different material to vitalize your creativity. And keep these tips in mind for freshening up your blog:

Acquire the reader feedback: There cannot be a better way to understand what the readers want to read than by asking them. You will find that the internet users are very responsive and acquiring their feedback will not be too difficult. These users will let you know the subjects they don't like and the ones they will like to discuss. It's possible to base your choice of subject on the number of users recommending it. It is a simple and effective way of knowing which blog content will be popular.

Select the right blogs for examining: Have you heard of angry blog syndrome? Ensure that you stay away from the blogs that are cynical about almost anything. These will not help in developing creativity. As a matter of fact these "angry" blogs affect your mentality in such a manner that your blog posts also begin to turn out in a similar manner. Refrain yourself from visiting these sites. Learn to judge which blogs are good and which are not. By studying the quality and recommended blogs you will learn what is necessary.

Have some other persons guest post on the blog: If you are running short of new ideas or just plain not in a mood to write, have someone guest blog on the blog. This is useful in building rapport with the users. Feature some user for supplying their very own post. This gradually builds the lifeline of your blog. The users feel more comfortable with your blog as it is like being their own.

And, in the end significantly, keep up the writing flow by just going at it again and again. Make note of the ideas and even note the mumblings. After some time it will become easier to write on any topic. Once you get in the flow of writing, it will become simpler to make money on internet.

-A STEP BY STEP GUIDE ON LEVERAGING YOUR POSTS FOR MAXIMUM ONLINE EXPOSURE

The first thing you can do is to find the right mixture of things that can help you get your work done. Previously you may have been working with a simple idea such as "How to start a Blog" and then building upon it like you did when you were an amateur. Now that you are swimming with the big fish, it is time to start acting like one too. Businesses will only buy your blog if you have got the right kind of audience following your every move, if you know what you are talking about and they know you have the ability to attract more attention every time you publish something new. It is all about going back to the basics of "How to start a Blog" and building upon it but with a manner of professionalism and business smarts.

The second thing to do is gain the trust of your readers. When you take the time out to write something, anything for an intended audience, the audience may just take the time out to read your blog. As a blogger, when you continually engage with them on a frequent basis, you could earn yourself a salary.

Thirdly, learn from your competitors and make sure you know where you lie on the landscape where every other company has their own famous blogger. Learn what they do best and make sure you can redo it but in a unique manner, learn from their lacking in any area and make sure you do not make the same mistake. Getting a company to sign you on to their team is harder than producing a fun loving blog. The actual blog structure and "How to start a Blog" without making any of the mistakes your competitors have made is the only goal to strive for. Companies can only purchase your blogs when you know "How to start a Blog" without their interventions. Therefore, be unique and make sure you know what, where when and "How to start a Blog" according to the situation and your topic. You should always know what you are supplying to the market and you should know what the audience wants. When you give them what they want, companies know you can sell their stuff and market them as well as yourself. By making your blogs a commodity, it is the way in which you can easily sell your blogs off and earn a good amount of cash.

Now you can earn a good amount of cash and be a professional blogger with companies who acknowledge you for your writing abilities and captivating skills that are attracting.

-PAY PER CLICK ADVERTISING AND SEARCH ENGINE OPTIMIZATION

If you're looking to drive more traffic to your website, then you've probably heard of the terms "pay per click advertising" and "search engine optimization" or "SEO." But what's the difference? And how does pay per click advertising (or PPC advertising) differ from search engine marketing or paid search?

Well, search engine marketing and paid search are really just euphemisms for pay per click advertising, which is also known as PPC advertising, or Google advertising because the majority of pay per click advertising runs on the Google search network, Google content network, and Google display network.

When you hear "pay per click advertising," think advertising. The listings generated from pay per click advertising are paid for, and they appear in the "sponsored links" sections at the very top and far right-hand side of search results pages. They can also appear on other websites that "lease" space to Google and other search engines to display advertising.

The words "pay per click" in the term pay per click advertising also tell us something. With pay per click advertising, the website owner pays a specific amount each time a user clicks on their ad. In other words, they pay per click, hence the name "pay per click advertising."

Pay per click advertising can be useful for advertisers who require highly-predictable marketing budgets. That's because pay per click advertisers control precisely how much they're willing to spend on their pay per click advertising. In fact, you can set a daily budget to ensure you never spend more than your company can afford.

Something else to consider about pay per click advertising is that each time an ad appears and a user doesn't click on it, there's no cost. Therefore, a pay per click advertising listing can appear thousands of times, be seen by thousands of internet users, and as long as no one clicks on it, the advertiser doesn't have to pay.

Of course, the goal of pay per click advertising is for users to click on ads, but it's helpful to know pay per click advertising can increase visibility even when users aren't clicking. This is especially useful when pay per click advertisers use banner ads, which are graphically-designed display ads that serve to internet users based on their search behavior.

By comparison to pay per click advertising, search engine optimization (SEO) is not advertising at all. Unlike pay per click advertising, SEO relies on your website's content, programming, and back-links to increase the likelihood your listing will appear among the top search results. But just because search engine optimization is not advertising, don't think SEO is free. In fact, an SEO program can cost as much or more than pay per click advertising. That's because effective SEO requires hiring an expert to modify your website's content and coding. In addition, effective

SEO programs require generating content and disseminating that content across the internet -- always with links back to your website. And all of this takes time and money.

On a more positive note, sophisticated internet users may be more likely to click on organic search results than on listings generated by pay per click advertising. The organic search results are listed below pay per click advertising results, and some internet users perceive these listings as more credible than pay per click advertising results.

Bottom line, both pay per click advertising and SEO are valuable and both should be part of your online marketing program. So if you want to increase visibility and traffic, make sure to set an adequate budget for pay per click advertising and SEO.

A website is the cheapest storefront you can ever purchase for your business. You do not have to pay rent and everything - from the cost of staff to the cost of inventory - is a fraction of what traditional businesses pay. But a storefront on the web does not mean much unless you have customers walking through your metaphorical front door. The quickest way to drive customers through the front door is pay per click advertising (also known as PPC). PPC places ads for your products and services on search engines like Google and social outlets like Facebook. When considering PPC for your business you have two options: go it alone and manage your own pay per click advertising campaign, or hire a pay per click advertising service. Neither one is an easy walk in the park.

Going It Alone

Pay per click can seem daunting for the uninitiated. Any business owner investigating the wilds of PPC for the first time will be confronted with the alphabet soup of terminology from Hell. "Bid management", "CPC", "Click Through Rate", "Keyword Planning", "Negative Keywords", and on and on and on. They will also find themselves in a thicket of terms of service and quality requirements. Google, for instance, has certain policies for each ad that must be abide by, or your ads will not be displayed.

Sound complicated? Yeah, because it is complicated. There is a reason that since the birth of PPC in the mid-2000s there has also been an accompanying explosion in pay per click advertising services that manage ad accounts. These pay per click management companies take the stress and time out of managing pay per click campaigns.

But not all pay per click advertising services are made of the same stuff. When looking at PPC Management companies you have a lot of choices. And picking the right type of Management Company will keep your business out of the woods.

PPC Management

PPC management agencies do exactly what the name implies; they manage your pay per click account for a percentage or a flat fee. Most often these agencies specialize in management for Google Adwords. In fact, Google encourages people to use agencies. They provide a Google Partners program where Adwords agencies can receive special benefits, like seminars and discounts.

Using pay per click advertising services for your business' website is a no-brainer. The brain-work comes into finding the right PPC management company for your company. There are several things to take into account. What kind of service do they offer? Do they manage just Adwords or do they also handle other PPC channels, like Facebook and Bing? What is their reporting like? Do they provide weekly, bi-weekly, or monthly reports?

The chief thing to look for in any marketing agency is how they respond to and treat you as a customer. Think of your PPC management company in the same way you think of your stockbroker. If you have a significant amount of money at a stock brokerage you would expect to call your and talk to your broker every week. You should expect that same level of service from your pay per click Management Company.

Pay per click advertising is the quickest way to drive traffic and business to your website. The key to effective PPC is not getting lost in the weeds and in most cases that means using an agency to manage your pay per click campaign.

Don't try to go it alone. Find a company that can help you maximize you pay per click advertising efforts. Still looking? Well, call us and we'll discuss how we can help you take advantage of your PPC campaign.

GETTING THE MOST FROM BANNER ADS

If you have spent more than 30 seconds online, chances are that you have seen banner ads. They are the advertising banners that are generally displayed at the sides and bottoms of websites and blogs. Ten years ago they were all the rage. The fact that much fewer people are using them today means that they can potentially be more effective in being able to promote your online business.

Advertising banners work best when they are targeted. What this means is that if you have an online business that sells dog-related products and services, you want to have your banner advertisements displayed on sites that are about dogs. It makes sense. If your banner ad that promotes your dog-related website is shown on a blog that's all about cats, chances are the conversion rates on your banner ad will be quite low.

Since proper targeting is key to the success of a banner advertisement campaign, how can you as an online business owner ensure that the banner ads that you create are placed in the best sites and blogs? How do you find sites that even provide banner advertising?

Banners Broker

www.bannersbroker.com/successwithguy

There are companies that act as middlemen in the banner advertising business. Banners Broker already have established relationships with owners of blogs and websites who do have available banner ads spaces. Not only do they have space reserved for banners ads, but they encompass hundreds of different niches and topics. Whichever niche that your online business is in, chances are that there are a number of possible places that you can immediately incorporate your advertising banners onto.

No need to go looking for sites and blogs in your niche that even use banner advertisements. No need to go searching for the contact information of webmasters and try to create a deal in which they will allow you to place your banner ads on their sites. The people at Banners Broker have already done the research and relationship-building for you. All you have to do is upload your banner code, select where you want it displayed, and choose how many impressions you want to have. It's just that simple.

And if you take advantage of their "free registration" today, you will get rewarded with 1000 free banner impressions. What better way to try out their services and see for yourself how effective banner advertising can be.

Banner advertising, when done alone, can be a very time-consuming and complicated process. That's the reason why so very few marketers opt to go that route. Instead, most online business owners use the services of a company like Banners Broker to handle all the ins and out of a successful banner ad marketing campaign.

Banner advertising, although it has slightly fallen out of favor for many marketers, is still an incredibly cost-effective way to reach are large number of people. The difference between a profitable campaign and one that loses money is the ability to place your banners in blogs and websites that are visited by people who would be most interested in the services and products you are offering. Banners Broker takes all the guesswork out of this process by already having those relationships established. As a online business owner, all the "work" that you need to do is simple and minimal.

Offline Traffic Generation

Is Offline Commissions a scam? This software tool has been programmed to help online marketers generate more income monetizing their sites more effectively. It is able to do this sending a continual stream of traffic to any website that they target from offline sources. Created by Adam Generale and Jacobo Benitez, this software combines the elements of both professional marketers' expertise.

What Are the Elements Behind the Creation of this Software and What Will It Help You Accomplish?

While Jacobo is mainly an expert in the field of maximizing conversions from new traffic, Adam is the one behind most of the offline traffic generation methods which have proven to be more targeted and more efficient to get than most online traffic sources. The end goal of this system is to help you set up your own 99% automated income stream as quickly as possible, skipping the steep learning curve typically required for beginners to get past before they can even see their first dollar online.

Free Lifetime Updates for All Members of Offline Commissions

Also, all members will get continual updates for free on all the latest happenings in the Internet marketing industry. Most importantly, you will want to make sure that your strategies do not get outdated and that you continually seek to improve your knowledge and methods to ensure that your competition does not get an edge over you.

What Can You Anticipate to Gain From Using this Traffic Generation Software?

By using this system, you will be learning both Adam's offline traffic generation strategies as well as Jacobo conversion methods. Both of these experts have individual courses that teach their strategies alone, therefore I am essentially getting 2 courses for the price of 1 when I follow this strategy.

By tapping into offline visitors, I have found myself getting a very good source of new traffic with very low competition, and this has greatly improved the amount of income that my sites are providing me with every month now.

CHAPTER 6

PERSONAL BRANDING

WHAT IS AN ONLINE PERSONAL BRAND?

Are you thinking about starting or have already started an internet business? Are you concerned in network marketing and need to use the web to grow your business? If that is the case there are 10 imperative factors that you need to grasp to guarantee your success.

Critical Factor 3 : Personal Branding

This one is enormous. Personal branding is going to play a critical role in how your message reaches your target audience. You MUST differentiate yourself in the marketplace, and the most important way to do that is thru personal Branding.

As our mom told us, there's nobody else quite like you, and it is correct. Your personal qualities and characteristic communicate who you are in an authentic way, folk need to know. All things being equal, folk will always decide to conduct business with people they know, like, and trust. All things not being equal, folks will still conduct business with those they know, like, and trust. Letting folk know who you are is a strong thing. It builds the reliability required for folk to want to do business with you.

In this process of working on your private brand, some particularly critical and sometimes difficult questions need to be asked. How does one plan to set apart yourself from the competition?

The fashion in which you respond these questions will help define your personal brand. This will identify you in the market, give a name and face to your promoting, and tells folks who you are and what you provide. This along with your unique selling offer will determine your marketing campaign.

An important part of making your personal brand is setting yourself up as a leader. When you offer valuable information and revelations to others, folks will begin to follow what you have to say. When they perceive you as a quality resource, you are positioning yourself in a leadership role. Being a teacher, coach, teacher, or anyone that brings helpful information and information to others is a powerful way to set apart yourself from your competition.

If your business is only getting started, your private brand won't be clear. That's to be expected. Your personal brand will develop and grow together with your business.

For those of us involved in the internet promotion industry, it is vital to make the difference between your private brand and your primary opportunity or business. The company you represent is not you. If you choose to change corporations, all of the company branding leaves with it. If you have a personal brand, your opportunity may change, but your private brand doesn't. Folks like to join folk they know, like and trust, and your personal brand builds that important relationship with your market that may last a whole life.

WHY SHOULD YOU MANAGE IT?

The process through which a positive reputation of for the online presence is maintained with the minimization of negative comments or information about a company is known as Online Reputation Management (ORM). Search Engine Optimization is primarily used to achieve this process. Online Reputation Management even proves helpful in Search Engine Marketing and Social Media Marketing.

Being humble is a principal concern for those who need to manage their online reputation. The overall reputation of any business is influenced by the way its online reputation is managed. When it comes to tackling negative publicity, whether it is from competitors or dissatisfied clientele, being prepared is necessary for businesses in a competitive market. Being prepared and ready is vital for online reputation management. In case of faults, humbly accepting them and if not diverting attention to positive points is the ideal way of tackling such a situation. The credibility of a business is never decreased if faults are publicly accepted. Instead, the authenticity and reliability of the online presence of a business is increased. Customers are mostly in search of responsible and trustworthy services, due to being well informed and since the market is so competitive.

Adequate responsibility on behalf of the company must be taken in the situation where something has been done to deserve the negative criticism. The fairness of a business actually becomes identifiable for the customers base by doing this. Even taking advantage of negative reviews and making them favorable for the business are also an important part of Online Reputation Management.

In online reputation management the reputation can be further damaged by angry counterattacks and reactions, which are rarely effective and only work in favor of the negative reviews. Quality expertise is required to deal with such situations. Thus, to take the responsibility of the online presence and reputation of a business, a dedicated PR team is necessarily needed. Not only can positive publicity be created by a PR team, but even negative publicity can be rectified as well.

For the growth of the online reputation of a business, SEO is also a significantly important part of online reputation management. Through Online Reputation Management, the following can be achieved:

The name of a business is spread across the online society and increased responses are generated.

Negative reviews are tackled and belittling attacks to the reputation of business, whether by competitors or and dissatisfied customers, are minimized.

A powerful online personal brand is created.

Social Media marketing and SEM are increased

The generation of positive traffic to online domains is increased.

ROI is increased with the generation of business.

For these varieties of reasons, for just about every business out there, online business reputation is of paramount importance.

ESTABLISHING CREDIBILITY

Any forum marketing expert will agree that user profile creation is fundamental in establishing an online presence. According to internet marketing gurus, forum marketing has proved to be a promotional arsenal that online business people have to seriously consider. This is mainly for internet business owners seeking to build an online image that will last.

In user profile formation it is significant that it be compelling. It is through your forum profile that you begin to establish credibility in your market niche. Here is where you should provide detailed description of your strengths as in experience and expertise. Do not hesitate to include personal content that will form a picture of how you are to your fellow business community members.

When you provide details like your favorite sport, name of your pet, where you come from or your best soccer team in your user profile creation, it ideally breaks the ice. In addition, this information humanizes you thus other forum members will have an imagination of your personality. However, avoid including polarizing content like your political inclination or religious beliefs. This will only lead to some individuals ignoring your posts.

Online business success is about implementing proper and working internet marketing strategies thus communication is imperative. Therefore, in the process of user profile creation remember to include your personal contact. This will enable other business community members reach you easily for more information about your business.

Remember to fill all required fields in the user profile creation process. In addition and also very importantly, use the same profile description in all the forum websites you register an account. This is how you eventually cut a niche for yourself hence build an online personal brand.

For more Valuable and Insightful Forum Marketing Tips click the links below, here you will also find more proven Online Marketing Ideas to better your online personal image.

HOW TO BUILD AN ONLINE PERSONAL BRAND

To start with ask yourself what you would like your brand to be. Many people mix up their brand with their job, or think that it is purely their professional competencies that make up their brand. There are a few more dimensions to it, like your values, and why you do what you do. This is a personal consideration, and something you should take your time with.

When you have written down your personal brand statement, spend some time and effort in social media. There are many websites for social media, but be aware that the emphasis is on "social", meaning that content must be interesting and original. Having outdated social media pages is almost worse than not having them at all. There are of course a few social media web pages that should be favored over others. LinkedIn, Twitter and Facebook are the most used, but be cautious how you use them, and how you interact with others.

What contributions should you make on social media websites? This is where you can stand out from the crowd, and talk about some unique perspectives, achievements, weird case studies or any circumstances where you used your professional skills. You can also write a little about yourself, like your community involvement, happenings in your area, or your travels. But unless you are focusing on a very specific target market, don't talk about questionable topics like politics, because controversy is most of the time a negative brand influence.

Along with investing time in social media, it is crucial to launch a personal website, with your full name in the URL. Not only does it give you total control over what you want to write (and not be worried about the guidelines of the social media sites), but it gives you the opportunity to have the website design that is unique to you and your brand. It also makes online promotion easier, especially if your name is competitive. Your website should have plenty of content that is relevant to your area of expertise. This is one domain that should be easy to find, and should have the type of high-quality content that builds you as an expert in your specialty.

Once you have recognized yourself and your brand on the internet with social media and your own web property, the next step is to promote yourself, and drive interested parties to your website and social media pages. By talking with other people on your social media platforms, but also at other places, like on blogs and in discussion forums, you will generate some interest if your contributions are interesting and valuable. Be careful not to promote yourself in social media, it is the equivalent of doing it at a birthday party, and in general will be seen as annoying, and will influence your brand negatively.

It is important to get started today. Your brand, like most other brands, will take time to become known and gain value, and needs ongoing work and reinforcement. Try these guidelines, and you will be seen as an authority in your field with a strong brand.

CONCLUSION

Building up a popular blog community could help if you want to make money online.

Once you have built a blog site, then it's time to get people to visit your blog and to keep on returning to it.

The tips bellow will help you to build a community around your blog that will ensure regular visitors and plenty of them.

Add great content to it. This is the most fundamental but necessary aspect to any successful blog site. If your content is not high quality, informative and engaging then you won't really get anywhere. It should be aimed at the reader and it should also provide solutions to issues that they could be dealing with currently.

Even if writing is not your forte, you can still add great content to your blog, but you may opt to outsource it. Another benefit of having great content is that it is more likely to get shared. This means that your readers will be doing your marketing for you, so it's well worth the effort. Your community will grow as friends and contacts promote your site for you.

An email subscriber list goes a long way with building your blog community. It provides you with the opportunity to stay in touch with your contacts and to also promote your products to a 'captive' market.

Just as long as your content is top quality, then you can rest assured that your email list will only expand.

Encourage comments. Blogs that contain calls to action for comments and sharing of further information help the building of a blog community. For example if you are providing a list of tips, then ask for readers to add to your tips. This way you'll be building the value of your information and you'll also build your community further.

Encourage interactions. You may decide to build a forum or you could host some competitions. However you decide to encourage interactions, they form part of the foundation of a dynamic community.

Build a presence on social media. Social media has made a massive impact on the internet over the last few years. It's part of the lifestyle of many people to regularly check their Facebook and/or Twitter newsfeeds.

By placing social media sharing buttons on your blog, you are enabling your readers to add your content to their news feeds and have your blog site and posts be discovered by more people.

Add a call to action for your readers to share your content if they found it useful - and by golly, go all out to make all of your content useful so that they will repay you by sharing it.

A lot of time and effort needs to go into creating a powerful blog community that will enable you to make an online income. It certainly won't happen overnight and is more of a marathon than a sprint.

By being committed and consistent with adding quality content, nurturing your community and by being grateful for any help that you receive along the way - you'll succeed.

So my last suggestion to you is to work on some really great content regularly and engage your readers by using the tips above. Your community will soon be supporting your growth and thriving. Then you truly would have succeeded in your quest to make an online income.

Thanks again for purchasing this book, I hope you enjoyed it!

CAN I ASK A FAVOUR?

If you enjoyed this book, found it useful or otherwise then I'd really appreciate it if you would post a short review on Amazon. I do read all the reviews personally so that I can continually write what people are wanting.

If you'd like to leave a review then please visit the Amazon store.

Thank you for your support!